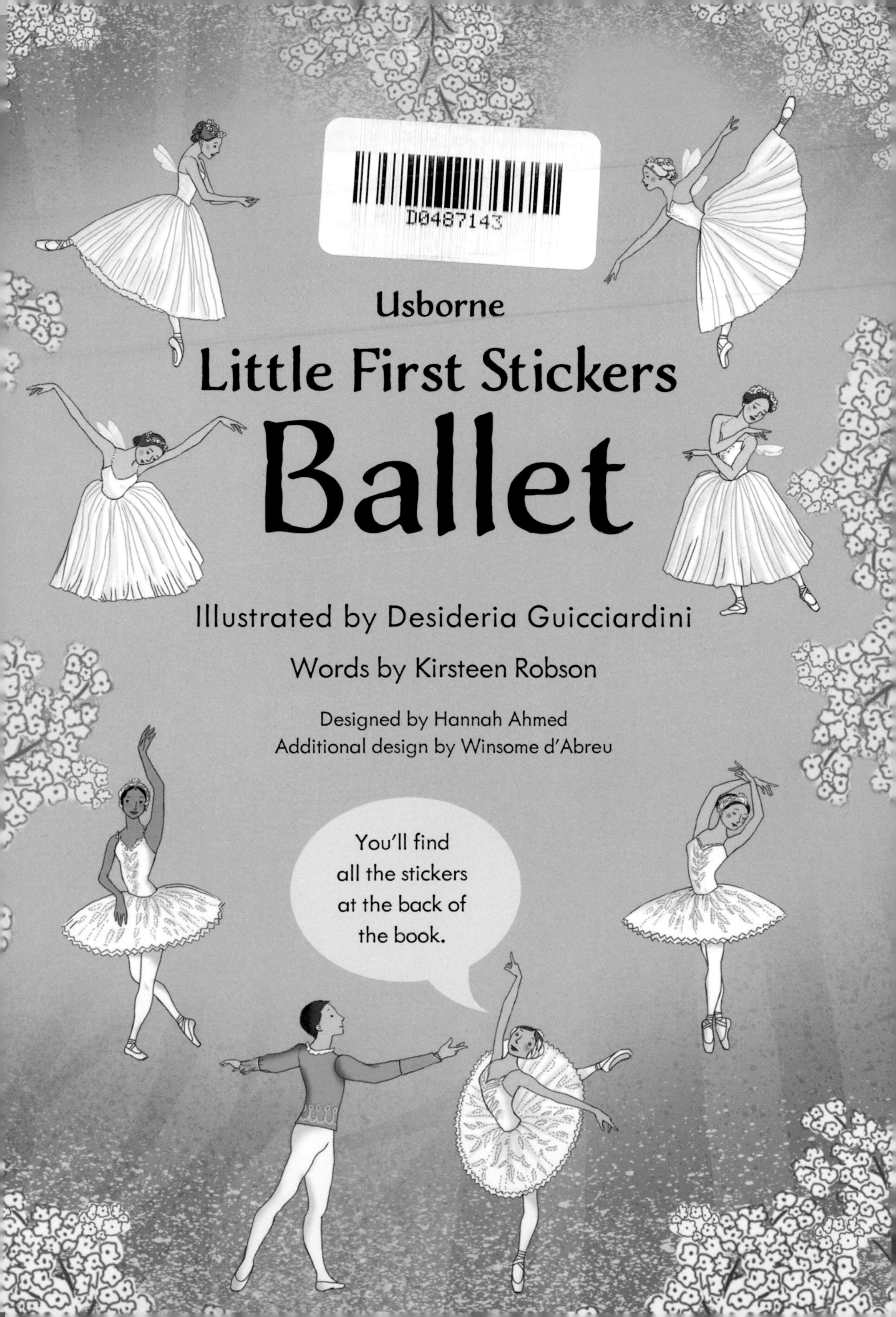

Usborne

Little First Stickers Ballet

Illustrated by Desideria Guicciardini

Words by Kirsteen Robson

Designed by Hannah Ahmed
Additional design by Winsome d'Abreu

Fairytale kingdom

Fill the castle garden with dancers dressed as characters from fairy tales.

In a class

Show some dancers working hard on the position of their arms and legs...

...and others perfecting
their leaps and jumps.

Moonlit lake

Stick the black swan on the lakeside with the prince in this scene from the ballet *Swan Lake*.

Then arrange a flock
of sparkly white swans
dancing around them.

Costume fitting

Dress the dancers
in the dazzling costumes
that best fit their poses.

Put the mannequin heads on the shelves and decorate them with masks, tiaras and wigs.

Magic at Christmas

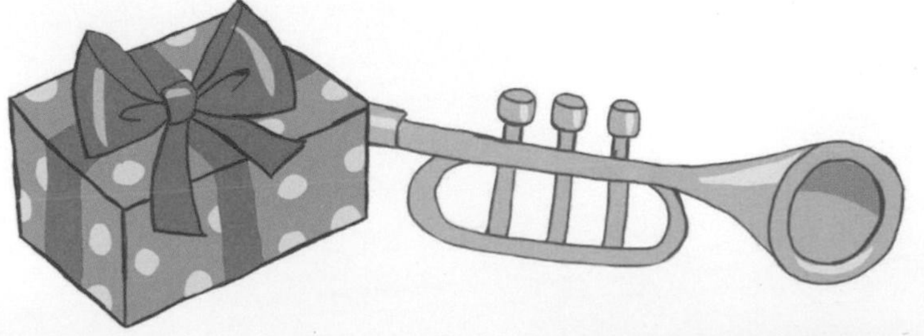

Show Clara helping toy soldiers fight a battle with rats in the Christmas ballet *The Nutcracker*.

A dollmaker's workshop

Fill the workshop with dancing dolls from the ballet *Coppélia*.

Rehearsal time

Arrange Cinderella and her
Fairy Godmother on the stage.

Then show the rest of the dancers
getting used to their costumes, props
and places as they rehearse *Cinderella*.

In an enchanted orchard

Create a scene from *The Firebird* ballet, placing the wicked magician in the orchard, with Prince Ivan and the Firebird who will defeat him.

Add the other dancers,
and then cover the trees
with golden apples.

The end of the show

Show the soloists bowing and curtseying, surrounded by roses thrown by their delighted audience.

Fairytale kingdom pages 2-3

In a class pages 4-5

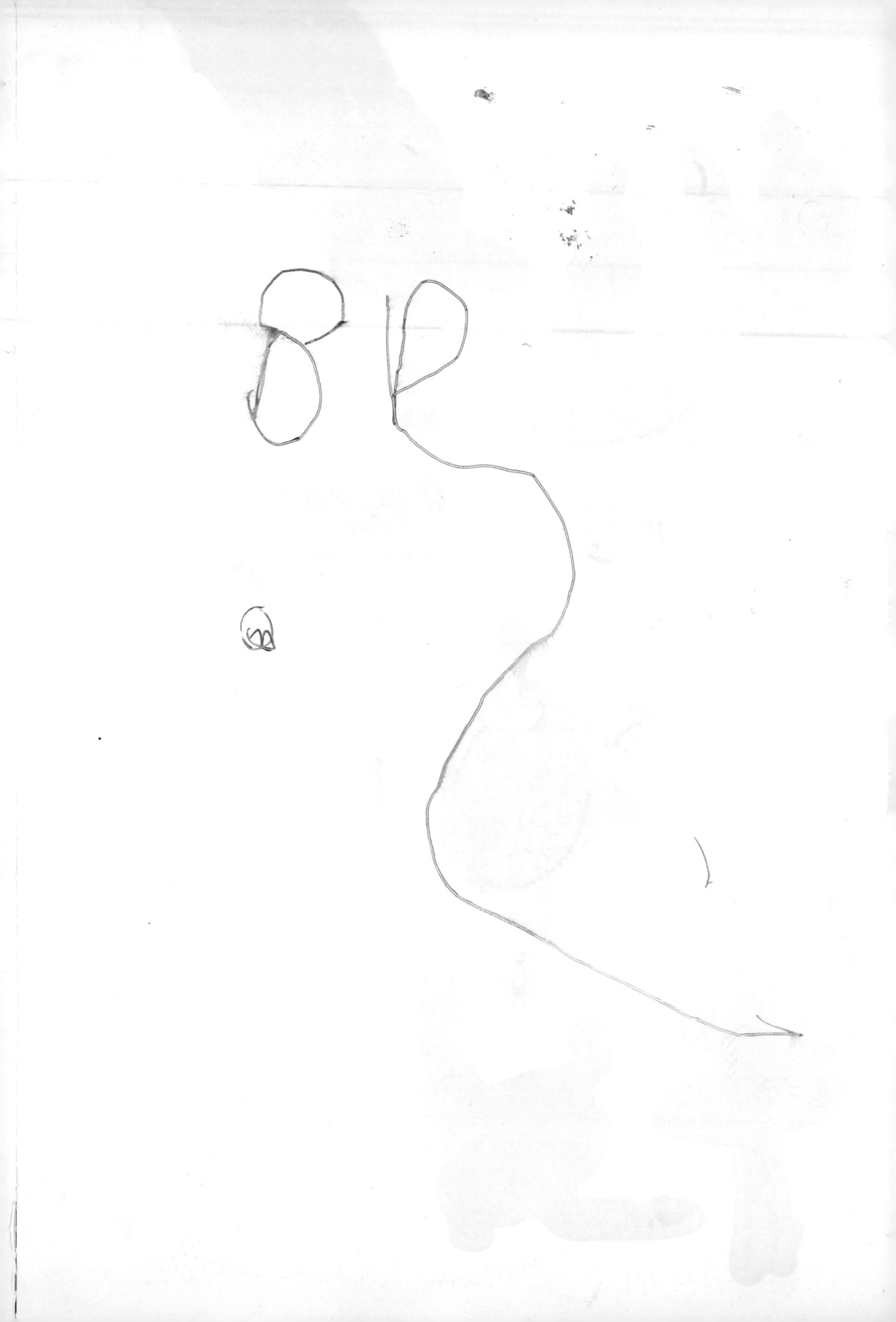

Moonlit lake pages 6-7

Costume fitting pages 8-9

Magic at Christmas page 10

A dollmaker's workshop page 11

Rehearsal time pages 12-13

In an enchanted orchard pages 14-15

The end of the show page 16